A Note to P

DK READERS is a compelling new program for beginning readers, designed in conjunction with leading literacy experts, including Dr. Linda Gambrell, Director of the School of Education at Clemson University. Dr. Gambrell has served on the Board of Directors of the International Reading Association and as President of the National Reading Conference.

Beautiful illustrations and superb full-color photographs combine with engaging, easy-to-read stories to offer a fresh approach to each subject in the series. Each DK READER is guaranteed to capture a child's interest while developing his or her reading skills, general knowledge, and love of reading.

The four levels of DK READERS are aimed at different reading abilities, enabling you to choose the books that are exactly right for your child:

Level 1 – Beginning to read
Level 2 – Beginning to read alone
Level 3 – Reading alone
Level 4 – Proficient readers

The "normal" age at which a child begins to read can be anywhere from three to eight years old, so these levels are intended only as a general guideline.

No matter which level you select, you can be sure that you are helping your child learn to read, then read to learn!

LONDON, NEW YORK, MUNICH,
MELBOURNE, AND DELHI

Project Editor Carey Combe
Art Editor Karen Lieberman
Senior Editor Linda Esposito
Senior Art Editor Andrew Burgess
US Editor Regina Kahney
Production Josie Alabaster
Picture Researcher Jamie Robinson
Illustrators Malcolm McGregor and
Peter Dennis

Reading Consultant
Linda B. Gambrell, Ph.D.

First American Edition, 1998
06 07 08 09 20 19 18 17 16 15
Published in the United States by DK Publishing, Inc.
375 Hudson Street, New York, New York 10014

Published in Great Britain by Dorling Kindersley Limited.

Library of Congress Cataloging-in-Publication Data
Dubowski, Cathy East.
    Shark Attack! / by Cathy East Dubowski. -- 1st American ed.
    p.   cm. -- (Dorling Kindersley readers. Level 3)
    Summary: Describes the nearly disastrous encounter of a spear
fisherman with a shark off the coast of Australia.
    ISBN-13: 978-0-7894-3440-1   ISBN-10: 0-7894-3440-7 (pbk)
    ISBN-13: 978-0-7894-3763-1   ISBN-10: 0-7894-3763-5 (hc)
    1. Shark attacks--Juvenile literature. [1. Shark attacks.]
I. Title. II. Series.
CL638-93.D825 1998
597.3' 15--dc21   98-14073
                                                         CIP
Color reproduction by Colourscan, Singapore
Printed and bound in China by L Rex Printing Co., Ltd.

The publisher would like to thank the following for their kind
permission to reproduce their images.
Key: a=above; c=center; b=below/bottom; l=left; r=right; t=top
Ardea London: Kev Deacon 11 b, 13; P. Morris 7; D. Parer & E.
Parer-Cook 19 tl; Ron & Valerie Taylor 11 c, 12, 15 cl, 18, 19 tr, 25 t,
28 b, 29 cl, br, 30 t, cl, 37 br, 38 c, 40 tr; Adrian Warren 19 b; **Bruce
Coleman Ltd:** Michael Glover 37 tr; **Mary Evans Picture Library:** 14
br; **The Ronald Grant Archive:** Jaws: The Revenge, 1987 ©
MCA/Universal Pictures 14 bl; **T. Britt Griswold:** 38 bl; **Innerspace
Visions:** Kurt Amsler 41 b; Bob Cranston 25 b; Nigel Marsh 40 bl;
Doug Perrine 46 t; **Oxford Scientific films:** Richard Herrmann 37 cl;
Pictor International: 41 tr; **Planet Earth Pictures:** F. J. Jackson 27;
Doug Perrine 15 b, 28 t, 42 cl; Marty Snyderman 10; James D. Watt
38–39, 47; Norbert Wu 15 cr; **Science Photo Library:** BSIP LECA 44;
Eye of Science 35; **Smithsonian Institution, NMNH:** Chip Clark 33
outer; **Waterhouse stock Photography:** Stephen Frink 45; **Wild
Images:** Howard Hall 31. Jacket: **Telegraph Colour Library:** main.
All other images © Dorling Kindersley.
For further information see: www.dkimages.com

Discover more at
www.dk.com

Contents

READING
3
ALONE

SHARK ATTACK!

Written by Cathy East Dubowski

DK Publishing, Inc.

Shark attack!

Rodney Fox had almost run out of time. He needed to find a big fish – and he needed to find it soon. The young Australian was competing in an annual spearfishing championship. To win he had to find and catch a big local fish. Rodney had won the contest last year, and he wanted to win again. But today something would happen. Something that would change his life forever.

Like all the other competitors in the contest, Rodney wore a line fixed to his dive belt to hold the fish he had caught.

Shark capital!
Australia has the highest number of shark attacks in the world. But even so, since 1901 there have been fewer than 300 attacks.

AUSTRALIA

He and the other divers had been diving for several hours. They had caught a lot of fish, and the water smelled of blood.

About half a mile (one km) offshore, Rodney spotted a huge morwong – just the fish he needed to win! Carefully, he aimed his spear gun at the fish.

CRASH! Something slammed hard into Rodney's side. He felt as if he had been hit by an express train!

It was a great white shark! The force of the impact knocked the mask off his face and the spear gun from his hand. His left shoulder disappeared down the creature's throat. Then the shark bit down on Rodney's chest and back.

Rodney struggled to get free. He hit the shark with his fist. But the shark held tight and shook him back and forth.

Then Rodney remembered the weakest spot on a shark's body – its eyes. With all his strength he rammed his right fist straight into the shark's eye. Incredibly, the shark let go.

Sharks' eyes

To protect its eyes from attack, a shark can roll them back into its head. Some sharks have a special membrane that covers the eyeball like a window shade.

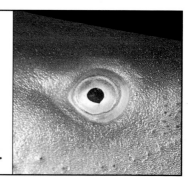

Bleeding and running out of air, Rodney struggled toward the surface. Could he make it to safety before the great white shark ate him alive?

Rodney reached the surface and gasped for air. He'd made it! But then he looked down. The shark was racing straight for him. Its huge jaws, lined with razor-sharp teeth, were wide open!

SNAP! The shark's jaws slammed shut again. But this time the shark swallowed the fish attached to Rodney's dive belt. Suddenly, Rodney felt himself being pulled through the water – he was still attached to the line!

The shark began to drag him down into deep water. He struggled to undo his dive belt, but the buckle had slipped around his back. He couldn't reach it.

Time was running out. If the shark didn't eat him, Rodney would drown.

Suddenly the line snapped. Rodney was free! He struggled to the surface and shouted for help. Luckily, friends in a nearby boat had seen the blood and quickly pulled him out of the water.

Rodney was seriously hurt. His rib cage, lungs, and the upper part of his stomach lay open from the huge gash where the shark had sunk its teeth in. The bite had crushed his ribs and punctured one of his lungs.

Rodney Fox is one of the few people to have survived the bite of a great white shark.

Rodney was rushed to the hospital. Four hours of surgery and 462 stitches saved his life. But he would wear the ugly scar of the shark's bite forever.

The attack on Rodney was big news. The public, frightened of more attacks, demanded action to clear the local beaches of sharks. But Rodney thought differently.

Deadly teeth

A shark's mouth has up to six rows of triangular teeth. When one tooth falls out, another takes its place. A great white shark has up to 100 teeth.

Rodney didn't want to go out and kill sharks – he wanted to go out and learn more about the mysterious creature that had nearly killed him. And he began a lifelong search to find out more about these silent hunters of the deep.

Only a few months after the attack, Rodney was diving again. So he could study sharks up close, Rodney designed and built the first shark cage.

Rodney Fox still dives with sharks, and is now trying to save them from extinction.

A shark cage is about the size of a small elevator car. It is made of very strong metal bars, which are placed close enough together to keep a shark from biting the divers inside but still allow the divers a good view of the shark. Floats at the top keep the cage from sinking.

Today many people use shark cages. They allow divers and scientists to study and photograph sharks close up – but not quite as close as Rodney once came! ❖

Shark attacks – the facts

If you're terrified of sharks, you're not alone. Shark attacks make frightening headlines, and movies like *Jaws* spread the fear that sharks are bloodthirsty killers. In fact, many people are scared just by the thought of sharks.

But the truth is that shark attacks are actually very rare. A person is far more likely to be hit by a car or struck by lightning than be attacked by a shark.

Popular fiction has helped spread false fears about sharks.

There are over 350 different species – or types – of sharks. And of these, only about 30 have ever been known to attack humans. But there are three that are really dangerous: the great white shark, the bull shark, and the tiger shark.

A tiger shark is large and powerful enough to attack most sea creatures.

Bull sharks are one of the few sharks that can live in both fresh and sea water.

The great white shark is the most feared and fearsome of all sharks. It has even been known to attack boats.

Whether or not you are in danger of a shark attack depends on where you live in the world. Sharks are found almost everywhere, but they seem to prefer warm water. Most shark attacks happen in Australia, Brazil, California, Florida, Hawaii, and South Africa. They often occur near crowded beaches where people go to swim, sail, and surf.

Almost all shark attacks take place in warm seas, as few sharks live in cold water.

▲ This symbol on the map shows the location of fatal shark attacks around the world.

PACIFIC OCEAN

NORTH AMERICA

ATLANTIC OCEAN

HAWAIIAN ISLANDS

SOUTH AMERICA

2000   4000   6000 km

But even in a very bad year, sharks attack no more than 80 to 100 people in the whole world. And modern transportation and medical care mean that only 10 to 15 of these people die.

Even then, sharks don't usually set out to attack people. Often they ignore people in the water. So what makes a shark attack a human?

Some people believe sharks attack when they feel threatened. A diver may unknowingly swim into a shark's territory. In this case, a shark may only bite a human once. It will then release – rather than eat – the invader. Perhaps this is what happened to diver Henry Bource. A single bite from a large shark resulted in him losing a leg. Divers are sometimes attacked while carrying fish they have caught. The blood and frantic movements of the dying fish attract sharks, who can smell blood from a great distance.

Henry Bource

A shark's view of a seal and a surfer from below

Sometimes a shark attack could be a case of mistaken identity. From a shark's point of view, a surfer on a surfboard looks like its favorite food – a seal. Once the shark has a taste of the board, it will spit it out and go away. Many surfers are still alive to tell the tale, with a munched surfboard to prove it!

This surfer's board was bitten by a 13-foot (4-meter) tiger shark in Hawaii.

An attack may happen because a shark is very hungry. Experts think that Raymond Short was attacked by a hungry shark while swimming in the water off a crowded Australian beach.

Raymond was swimming near the shore when he was bitten by a shark. Six lifesavers immediately dashed into the sea to save him. But as they started to carry Raymond toward the shore the lifesavers realized the shark was still attached to Raymond's leg!

Raymond had
to be pulled right
onto the beach
before the shark
let go of his leg.

The shark had a long wound along
its stomach. It had been badly injured.
Scientists think the shark had been
unable to catch its normal food and
was so hungry it took unusual risks.

Another strange attack took place in a very unexpected place – a creek!

Twelve-year-old Lester Stilwell was swimming with his friends in Matawan Creek in New Jersey. Suddenly he screamed and disappeared beneath the water. A man named Stanley Fisher rushed into the creek to drag Lester's lifeless body from the water. Suddenly Stanley felt something bump his right leg. When he reached down he realized part of his leg had been ripped away.

They had been attacked by a shark! Tragically both died from their wounds.

Was this attack really so strange? Not if you know about sharks. Even though the shark was never found, it was most likely a bull shark, a species that lives in both salt and fresh water. ❖

Sharks and safety

People have tried many ways to protect themselves from shark attacks as they explore the shark's watery world.

One of the most popular methods of protecting swimmers is simply to build a fence, or shark net, in the water. These shark nets are used off many popular Australian and South African beaches.

Shark nets are set up off popular beaches.

Nets stop sharks from swimming into an area.

But the nets cost a lot of money to build and need to be repaired often.

Electrical beach barriers are also being tested, as sharks won't swim through strong electric currents.

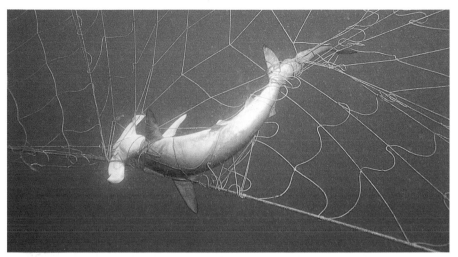

A big problem with shark nets is that they trap and kill all types of sharks, as well as other creatures like dolphins.

How to avoid a shark attack:

- Never swim by yourself.
- Don't swim if you have a cut. Sharks can smell blood a mile (1.6 km) away.
- Don't swim at dusk, as this is the time when sharks are likely to be feeding.
- Don't urinate in the sea. Sharks are attracted to the smell.
- Get out of the water if a shark is seen in the sea.

MUNICIPALITY OF ROCKDALE

DANGER

SHARKS IN BOTANY BAY

People who are victims of shipwrecks or plane crashes at sea are often at risk of being attacked by a shark because they are so far from land.

One invention to protect people floating in the sea is the shark screen bag. It is like a large plastic bag, which is closed at the bottom and has floats at the top. When not in use, it is small enough to be folded up and tucked into a pocket. But when inflated, the bag hides the person's shape, movement, smells, and sounds from passing sharks, hopefully keeping the person safe until help arrives.

Many people have tried to invent a chemical shark repellent. During World War II many soldiers were killed by sharks when their ships sank. The army tried to make a repellent made of chemicals and dye. It was meant to repel sharks and hide the person from the shark. But it didn't work, as it melted too quickly.

One of the latest ideas is to try to copy the poison made by a fish called the moses sole. If caught by a shark, the fish squirts out poison. Sharks hate the taste so much, they spit the fish out!

A moses sole swims so slowly, it protects itself with poison.

Divers who dive for sport or to study and film underwater life often come face to face with dangerous sharks. Some carry spear guns, or bangsticks that fire a small explosive charge that can kill a shark. But for those who want to study sharks, killing them is not the answer.

A bangstick is more effective than a spear gun against a large shark.

Valerie and Ron Taylor developed a new idea. These Australian filmmakers are well known for their underwater photography. But it is dangerous work. Valerie has the shark bites to prove it!

On one dive trip, the Taylors noticed a crew member wearing some stainless-steel mesh gloves to protect his hands while cleaning fish. This gave them an idea. Why not make a whole dive suit out of chain-mail to protect divers from sharks – like the chain-mail suits worn by knights?

They made a suit out of 400,000 tiny stainless-steel rings. But to test the suit, someone had to wear it in the water. Someone had to make the sharks bite!

Saving their skins
Small rings on a chain-mail suit stop a shark's teeth from biting through skin. But the diver will still be bruised.

Valerie in her chain-mail suit

The Taylors carried out a test dive off the coast of California. Raw chunks of fish were dumped into the water to attract sharks. Valerie Taylor zipped up the chain-mail suit over her regular dive suit and then dived into the water among the raw chunks of fish.

Soon several sharks darted in. Valerie waved a bleeding fish close to her body, baiting the sharks to bite. Suddenly a shark chomped down on Valerie's arm! She was startled, but not hurt.

The shark bit her again and again all over her body. It was frightening, but the shark's teeth couldn't get through the mesh. The suit had worked!

But it wasn't all so easy. At one point, a shark pulled off one of Valerie's gloves and bit her thumb. Valerie managed to fight off the shark and get away to safety.

The suit needed small improvements. But thanks to Valerie's bravery, the first practical shark suit had been invented! ❖

Diver protected from a shark attack by his chain-mail suit

Sharks up close

Sharks have roamed the earth's oceans for nearly 400 million years and are 200 million years older than the dinosaurs! But today's sharks are a lot like their early ancestors.

The biggest of these ancient sharks was called the *Carcharodon megalodon* (car-CARE-oh-don MEG-a-loh-don). This shark's huge jaws were over 6 feet (1.8 meters) wide. It weighed up to 10,000 pounds (4,535 kilograms) and grew to 54 feet (16 meters). That's twice as long as today's great white shark.

Fearsome fossils

Many early sharks left fossilized imprints when they fell to the bottom of the sea and were covered in sand. Often, the hard parts like spines and teeth were also fossilized.

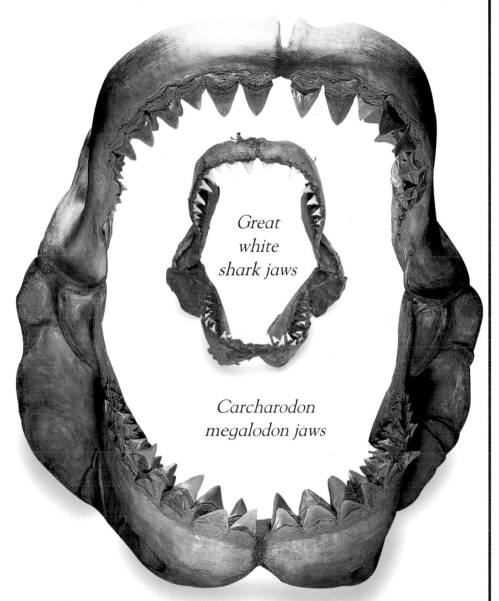

Great white shark jaws

Carcharodon megalodon jaws

Those early sharks died out. But life in the sea has changed very little, and today's sharks can tell us a lot about the animals that lived millions of years ago.

The shark is perfectly evolved for surviving and hunting underwater. Its amazingly flexible body is due to a skeleton made of cartilage – the same material that forms our noses and ears!

A shark has the same five senses as a human – sight, hearing, smell, taste, and touch. But the shark's ability to catch prey in murky waters is due to two extra, and very unusual, senses.

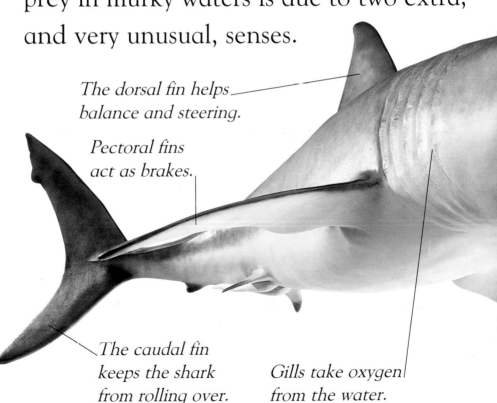

The dorsal fin helps balance and steering.

Pectoral fins act as brakes.

The caudal fin keeps the shark from rolling over.

Gills take oxygen from the water.

The "lateral line" is a series of invisible pressure-sensitive organs on each side of a shark's body. These help the shark sense very small vibrations in the water.

On the head of a shark are tiny pores called the ampullae of Lorenzini (am-POOL-ee of lor-un-ZEE-nee). They allow a shark to sense the faint electrical charges given off by all living things.

Sharks can hear up to 1,000 feet (305 meters).

Sharks can see up to 50 feet (15 meters) away.

Ampullae of Lorenzini

Shark skin

Shark skin is covered with tiny tooth-like scales. Before sandpaper, shark skin was used to smooth down wood!

Sharks are solitary animals – they live, swim, and hunt alone. Scientists know very little about their life cycle. What is known, however, is that sharks are very slow to reproduce. Some sharks take 11 years before they are ready to mate. And when sharks do give birth, they often have few babies. So sharks take extra care to protect their eggs.

Many lay their eggs in tough protective egg cases. Others give birth to live babies called pups. To help them survive these pups are already quite big when they are born.

Egg cases

Shark pups

Sharks eat most kinds of food – but all sharks eat meat. Many eat small fish and animals like jellyfish and lobsters,

Basking shark

although tin cans and plastic bags have also been found in a shark's stomach! Some larger sharks hunt bigger animals,

Jellyfish

such as seals, penguins, and even other sharks. A few, like the basking shark, simply swim along with their mouths wide open. They catch plankton, the tiny plant and animal life in the ocean as well as small animals such as shrimps.

Seals

Do you think you know what a shark looks like? Maybe you should think again! When most people think of sharks, they imagine the great white. But sharks come in all sizes and some very unusual shapes. Just look at the angel shark, the horn shark, the hammerhead shark, and the wobbegong!

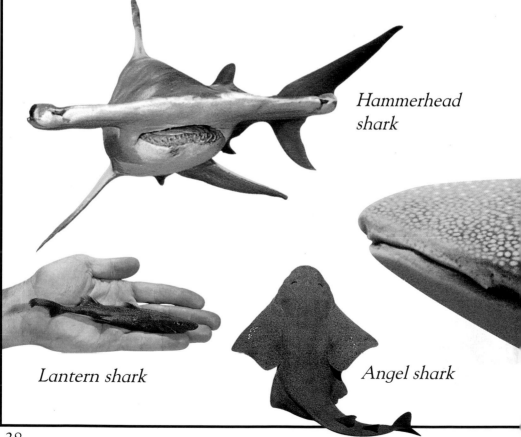

Hammerhead shark

Lantern shark

Angel shark

The biggest shark is the whale shark. It can grow up to 40 feet (12.2 meters) long and weigh as much as 13 tons, (13.2 tonnes) making it the largest fish in the world. One of the smallest sharks is the lantern shark. It grows no larger than 8 inches (20 centimeters) long! It is known as the lantern shark because its eyes glow in the dark! ❖

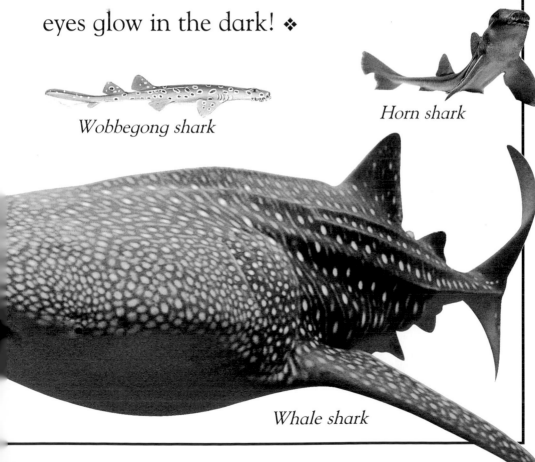

Wobbegong shark

Horn shark

Whale shark

Sharks under attack

For centuries people have feared sharks. But, today, sharks have much more to fear from people. Overfishing is threatening many species with extinction.

Shark's tooth necklace

Sharks have been hunted for many years. Their flesh and teeth were used for weapons, food, and even jewelry. But the numbers caught posed no threat to the shark population. Today, modern fishing methods mean that sharks are killed in huge numbers – up to 100 million sharks each year. As a result, the population of some sharks may have dropped by as much as 80 percent in the last ten years.

Often the sharks are killed by accident because they get trapped in fishing nets. The fishermen keep the fish they want and throw the unwanted sharks back into the ocean – dead.

Much shark killing is just for sport. People who hunt and kill a shark may seem brave, but they are never in any danger. The jaws make flashy trophies that sell to tourists for lots of money.

This shark hunter hangs his victims' jaws around his boat.

Shark meal

Sharks are also under attack because, in many parts of the world, people eat shark meat. In Asia, shark-fin soup is an expensive treat. Fishermen can earn so much money from shark fins that, when they catch a shark, they hack off its fins and throw the dying animal back into the water.

Fins from any type of shark are used to make shark-fin soup.

In some countries shark cartilage is made into health pills. Some people believe that the pills will cure almost anything, from heart disease to cancer. Nearly all of these claims are false.

Shark skin is also tanned and made into very expensive leather belts and wallets.

Modern shark leather box

One of the most valuable shark products is its liver. The oil taken from a shark's liver is used in many products, including industrial oils and medicines. The oil was also used to make vitamin A pills until a different source was found in the 1950s.

Vitamin A tablets

Cruel creams

The gall bladder and liver of sharks are still used to make beauty creams, even though natural plant oils could be used instead.

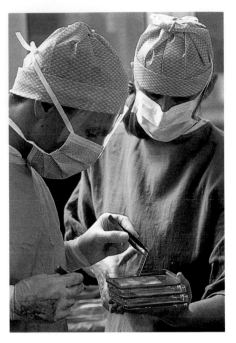

Doctors with artificial skin grown from shark cartilage

If we don't control the mass killing of sharks, they may become extinct. But why would this matter?

Scientists have discovered many amazing things about sharks, and we have a great deal to learn from this ancient creature. Sharks may even save our lives one day.

For instance, researchers have found that squaline, a chemical found in the liver and stomach of the dogfish shark, slows down the growth of tumors in people. And shark cartilage is now used to make artificial skin for burn patients.

Sharks also have highly developed immune systems -- which means they don't often get sick. Their cuts and wounds heal very fast. And they rarely get cancer like some animals can, even when scientists inject cancer cells into the sharks' bodies in the laboratory.

Why? Scientists don't know yet. But studying sharks may help doctors cure people who are sick.

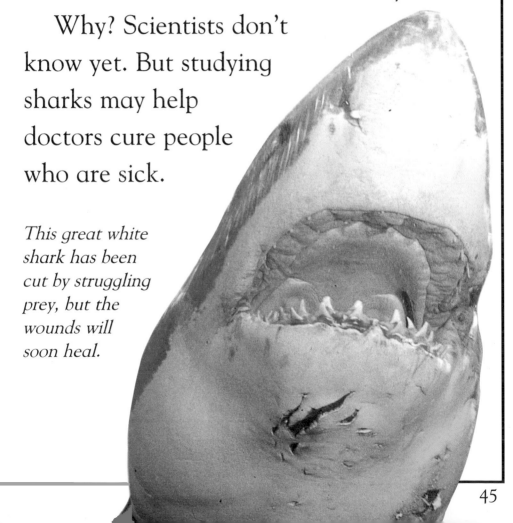

This great white shark has been cut by struggling prey, but the wounds will soon heal.

Aquariums are safe places to go and see a shark!

The more we learn about sharks, the more we will learn to admire and respect them. Of course most people don't want to come face to face with a great white shark in the ocean – like Rodney Fox!

But we can visit sharks in aquariums and watch fascinating films made by underwater filmmakers. We can even take trips to see sharks in the sea.

Sharks are fascinating, intelligent, and graceful creatures. Only a few kinds of sharks are dangerous. Attacks on people are really very rare. The shark's reputation as a bloodthirsty killer is not accurate or fair.

Sharks have had a home on our planet far longer than we have. It would be a shame if people made them disappear from our seas forever. ❖

Glossary

Ampullae of Lorenzini
(am-POOL-ee of lor-un-ZEE-nee)
Tiny pores on a shark's head that can detect faint electrical signals in the water.

Aquarium
A large tank where sea animals are kept so people can view them safely.

Bangstick
An underwater gun that fires a small explosive charge that is strong enough to kill a large shark.

Carcharodon megalodon
(car-CARE-oh-don MEG-a-loh-don)
The largest shark that ever lived in the sea. It died out over 10 million years ago.

Cartilage
A tough, flexible material from which a shark's skeleton is made. Human noses and ears are also made of cartilage.

Chain-mail suit
A dive suit made up of thousands of tiny interlocking stainless-steel rings. It protects divers from shark bites.

Denticles
The tiny tooth-like scales that cover a shark's skin.

Extinction
When a particular animal or plant dies out completely.

Fossils
The remains of plants and animals that lived millions of years ago. Fossils are often in rocks.

Lateral line
A line of invisible points on each side of a shark's body that help sharks sense vibrations in the water.

Moses sole
A slow fish that releases a poisonous liquid when caught.

Plankton
Tiny animals and plants that live in the sea.

Shark cage
A small metal cage that protects divers.

Shark chaser
A mix of chemicals and dye shaped into a cake. It was meant to protect people from sharks.

Shark net
A net that is hung under the water to stop sharks from reaching swimmers off a beach.

Shark screen bag
An inflatable bag that hides shipwreck victims from sharks by hiding any smells or movements.

Spearfishing
Fishing underwater with a spear gun.

Spear gun
An underwater gun that fires spears. It is used by underwater divers to catch fish.

Squaline
A valuable chemical found in a shark's liver. Humans use it for a number of medical reasons.